easy **MANDOLIN TAB EDITION**

JUST FOR FUN

CLASSIC ROCK MANDOLIN

12 GREAT SONGS OF THE '60S, '70S, & '80S

ARRANGED BY ANDREW DUBROCK

Alfred

Produced by
Alfred Music Publishing Co., Inc.
P.O. Box 10003
Van Nuys, CA 91410-0003
alfred.com

Printed in USA.

ISBN-10: 0-7390-6458-4
ISBN-13: 978-0-7390-6458-0

Cover Photos
Central image models: Katrina Hruschka and Andrew Callahan / Photographer: Brian Immke, www.adeptstudios.com
Mandolin: courtesy of Gibson USA • Moon: courtesy of The Library of Congress • Gramophone: © istockphoto / Faruk Tasdemir
MP3 player: © istockphoto / tpopova • Microphone: © istockphoto / Graffizone • Handstand: © istockphoto / jhorrocks
Jumping woman: © istockphoto / Dan Wilton • Woman and radio: courtesy of The Library of Congress • Sneakers: © istockphoto / ozgurdonmaz
Background: image copyright Elise Gravel, 2009, used under license from Shutterstock.com

 Contents printed on 100% recycled paper.

FOREWORD

Classic Rock Mandolin is designed for your total enjoyment.
Each song uses the original guitar parts arranged for the mandolin.
Make sure to listen to the original recordings so you know how these
parts should sound before you start trying to learn them. Also, check
out the many examples of excellent mandolin playing on YouTube.
But most important, just have fun!

—Aaron Stang, Editor
Alfred Music Publishing Co., Inc.

CONTENTS

AFTER MIDNIGHT

Moderately fast rock

Words and Music by
J.J. CALE

Af - ter mid - night,_____ we gon' let it all_____ hang_____ down.

Af - ter mid - night,_____ we gon' shake your tam - bou - rine.

GO YOUR OWN WAY

Words and Music by
LINDSEY BUCKINGHAM

1. Lov - ing you   is - n't the right___   thing_ to do.
2. Tell__ me why   ev - 'ry-thing turned_   a - round.
(3.) *Guitar Solo*

How_ can I___   ev__ er change
Pack - ing up,___   shack - ing up's

things_ that_ I feel?_____   If__ I could,___
all__ you wan - na do.   If__ I could,___

Go Your Own Way - 3 - 1

Go Your Own Way - 3 - 2

⊕ *Coda*

Chorus:

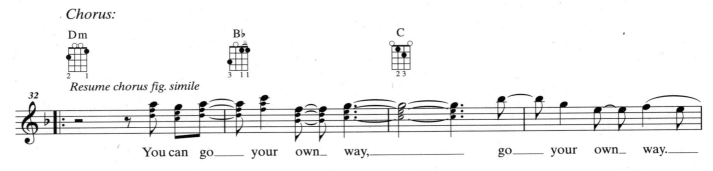

You can go___ your own___ way,_____ go___ your own___ way._____

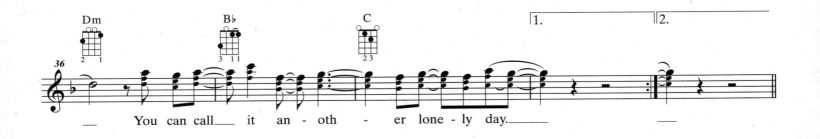

___ You can call___ it an - oth - er lone - ly day._____

Instrumental:

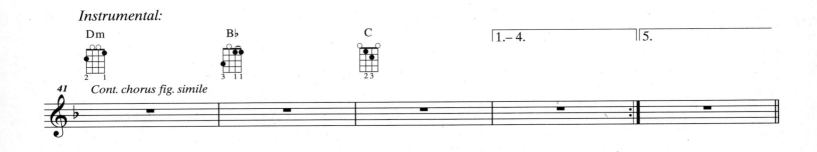

Chorus:

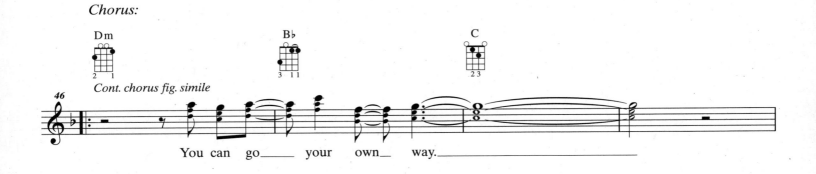

You can go_____ your own___ way._____

Repeat and fade

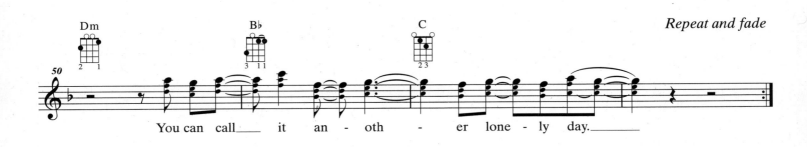

You can call___ it an - oth - er lone - ly day._____

IT'S ALL OVER NOW

It's All Over Now - 3 - 1

Chorus:

used to___ love her,   but it's all___ o - ver now.___

Be-cause I   used   to___   love her,   but   it's   all___   o - ver now.___

To Coda ⊕ | 1. | | 2.

w/verse rhy. simile

2. Well,   she

Guitar Solo:

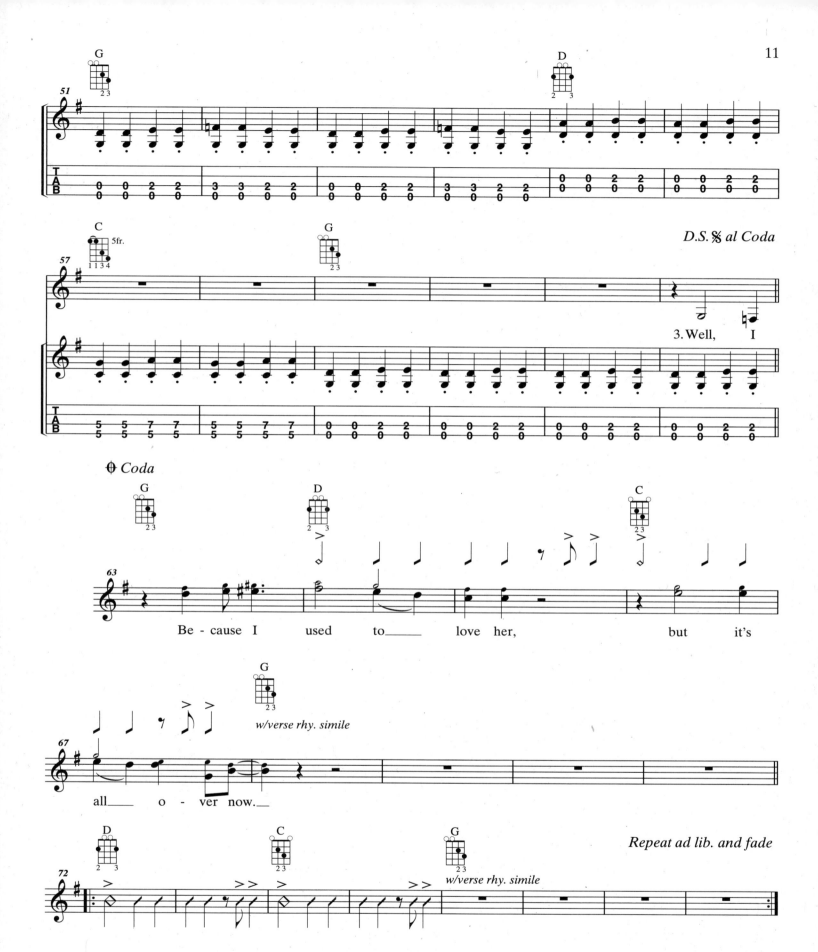

Verse 3:
Well, I used to wake in the morning, get my breakfast in bed.
When I'd gotten worried, she'd ease my aching head.
But now she's here and there with every man in town,
Still trying to take me for that same old clown.
(To Chorus:)

HOTEL CALIFORNIA

Words and Music by
DON HENLEY, GLENN FREY
and DON FELDER

Verse 3:
Mirrors on the ceiling, the pink champagne on ice.
And she said, "We are all just prisoners here of our own device."
And in the master's chambers they gathered for the feast.
They stab it with their steely knives but they just can't kill the beast.
Last thing I remember I was running for the door.
I had to find the passage back to the place I was before.
"Relax," said the nightman, "We are programmed to receive."
You can check out anytime you like but you can never leave.

JUMP

Words and Music by EDWARD VAN HALEN, ALEX VAN HALEN,
MICHAEL ANTHONY and DAVID LEE ROTH

18

Jump - 3 - 3

LONG TRAIN RUNNIN'

Words and Music by
TOM JOHNSTON

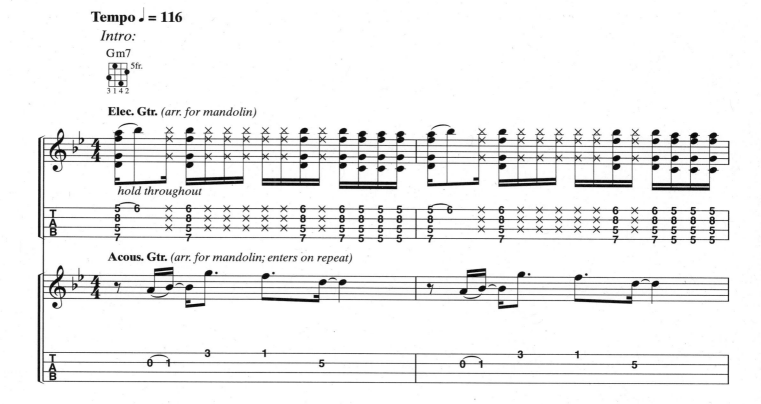

Long Train Runnin' - 3 - 1

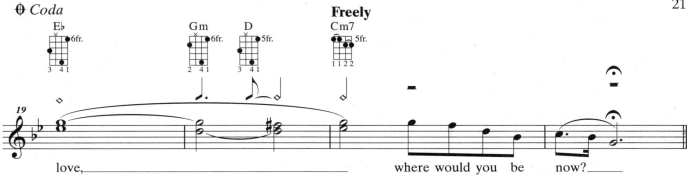

love,_____ where would you be now?_____

Repeat ad lib. and fade

Verse 2:
You know I saw Miss Lucy,
Down along the tracks;
She lost her home and her family,
And she won't be comin' back.
Without love, where would you be right now,
Without love?

Verses 3 & 5:
Well, the Illinois Central
And the Southern Central freight,
Gotta keep on pushin', mama,
'Cause you know they're runnin' late.
Without love, where would you be right now,
Without love?
(1st time to Verse 4:)
(2nd time to Verse 6:)

Verse 4:
Instrumental Solo
(To Verse 5:)

Verse 6:
Where pistons keep on churnin'
And the wheels go 'round and 'round,
And the steel rails are cold and hard
For the miles that they go down.
Without love, where would you be right now,
Without love?
(To Coda)

MAGGIE MAY

Words and Music by
ROD STEWART and MARTIN QUITTENTON

Moderately ♩ = 130

1. Wake up, Mag-gie, I___ think I got some-thing to say to you.___ It's

2.3.4. *See additional lyrics*

late Sep - tem - ber and I real - ly should_ be back__ at__ school. I

know I keep you a - mused,___ but I feel I'm be - ing used.___ Oh,

Maggie May - 4 - 1

*D/F♯ 2nd and 3rd time only.

Mag-gie, I could-n't have tried__ an-y-more._____ You led me a-way from__ home just to save you from be-ing a-lone. You stole my heart__ and that's__ what real-ly hurts.__ 2. The

Guitar Solo 1:

D.S. 𝄋 al Coda

⊕ *Coda*   *Guitar Solo 2:*

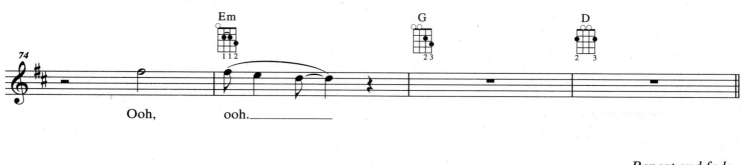

Ooh, ooh._____

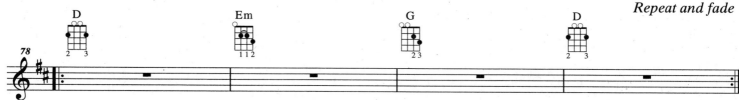

Repeat and fade

Verse 2:
The morning sun, when it's in your face,
Really shows your age.
But that don't worry me none,
In my eyes you're everything.
I laughed at all of your jokes,
My love you didn't need to coax.
Oh, Maggie, I couldn't have tried anymore.
You lead me away from home
Just to save you from being alone.
You stole my soul and that's a
Pain I can do without.

Verse 3:
All I needed was a friend
To lend a guiding hand.
But you turned into a lover and, mother,
What a lover, you wore me out.
All you did was wreck my bed,
And in the morning kick me in the head.
Oh, Maggie, I couldn't have tried anymore.
You lead me away from home
'Cause you didn't want to be alone.
You stole my heart,
I couldn't leave you if I tried.
(To Guitar Solo 1:)

Verse 4:
I suppose I could collect my books
And get on back to school.
Or steal my daddy's cue,
And make a living out of playing pool.
Or find myself a rock and roll band
That needs a helping hand.
Oh, Maggie, I wish I'd never seen your face.
You made a first-class fool out of me,
But I'm as blind as a fool can be.
You stole my heart
But I love you anyway.
(To Guitar Solo 2:)

THE NIGHT THEY DROVE OLD DIXIE DOWN

Moderate rock ballad ♩ = 132

Words and Music by
J. ROBBIE ROBERTSON

1. Vir - gil Caine is the name and I served
2.3. *See additional lyrics*

on the Dan - ville train, 'til Stone - man's cav - al - ry came and tore up the tracks a - gain.

In the win - ter of 'six - ty - five, we were hun - gry, just bare - ly a - live. By May the tenth, Rich-mond had fell; it's a time I re - mem - ber oh, so well. The

The Night They Drove Old Dixie Down - 3 - 1

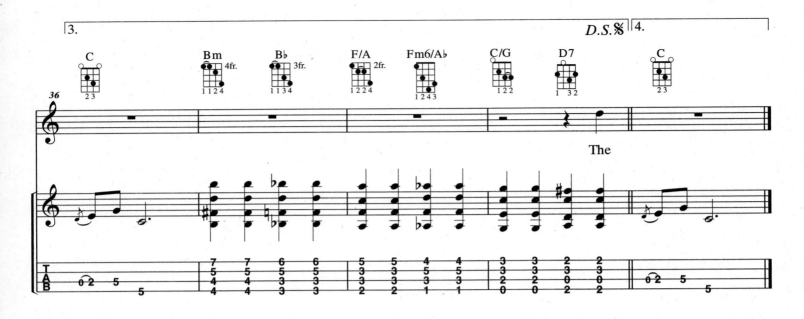

The

Verse 2:
Back with my wife in Tennessee,
One day she called to me,
"Virgil, quick come see,
There goes the Robert E. Lee."
Now, I don't mind choppin' wood,
And I don't care if the money's no good.
You take what you need and you leave the rest
But they should never have taken the very best.
(To Chorus:)

Verse 3:
Like my father before me,
I will work the land.
And like my brother above me,
Who took a rebel stand;
He was just eighteen, proud and brave,
But a Yankee laid him in his grave.
I swear by the mud below my feet,
You can't raise a Caine back up when he's in defeat.
(To Chorus:)

PAINT IT, BLACK

Paint It, Black - 3 - 1

30

Verse 3:
I look inside myself and see my heart is black.
I see my red door, I must have it painted black.

Bridge 3:
Maybe then I'll fade away and not have to face the facts.
It's not easy facing up when your whole world is black.

Verse 4:
No more will my green sea go turn a deeper blue.
I could not foresee this thing happening to you.

Bridge 4:
If I look hard enough into the setting sun,
My love will laugh with me before the mornin' comes.
(To Verse 5:)

STAIRWAY TO HEAVEN

Slowly ♩ = 72
Intro:

Words and Music by
JIMMY PAGE and ROBERT PLANT

34

Stairway to Heaven - 8 - 3

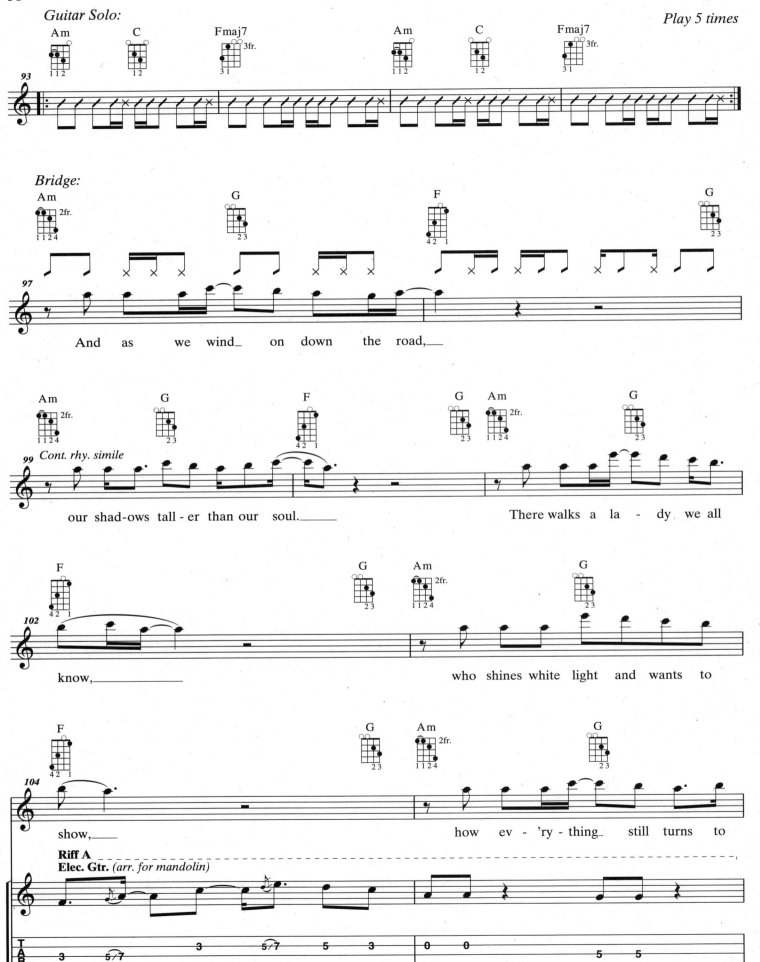

SUNSHINE OF YOUR LOVE

Words and Music by
JACK BRUCE, PETE BROWN
and ERIC CLAPTON

Moderately ♩ = 114

Intro:

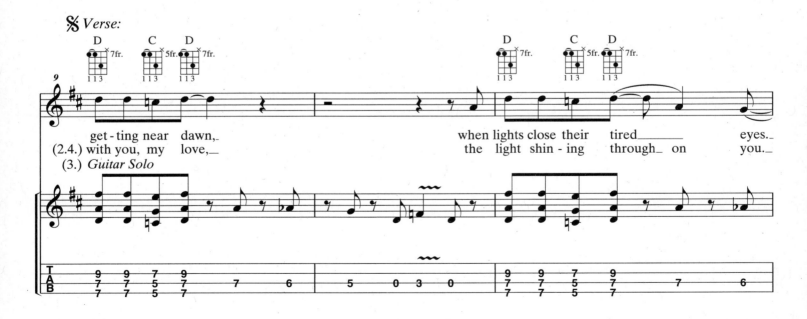

Sunshine of Your Love - 4 - 1

42

TRUCKIN'

Words by ROBERT HUNTER
Music by JERRY GARCIA,
BOB WEIR and PHIL LESH

48

Truckin' - 5 - 5

A CHORDS

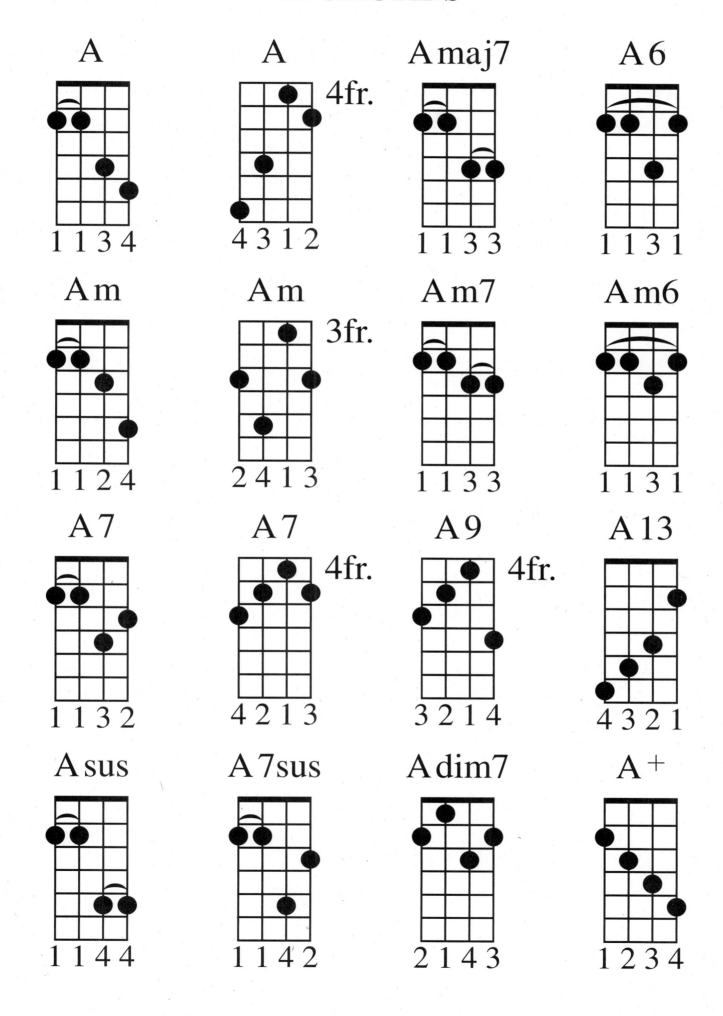

B♭ (A♯) CHORDS*

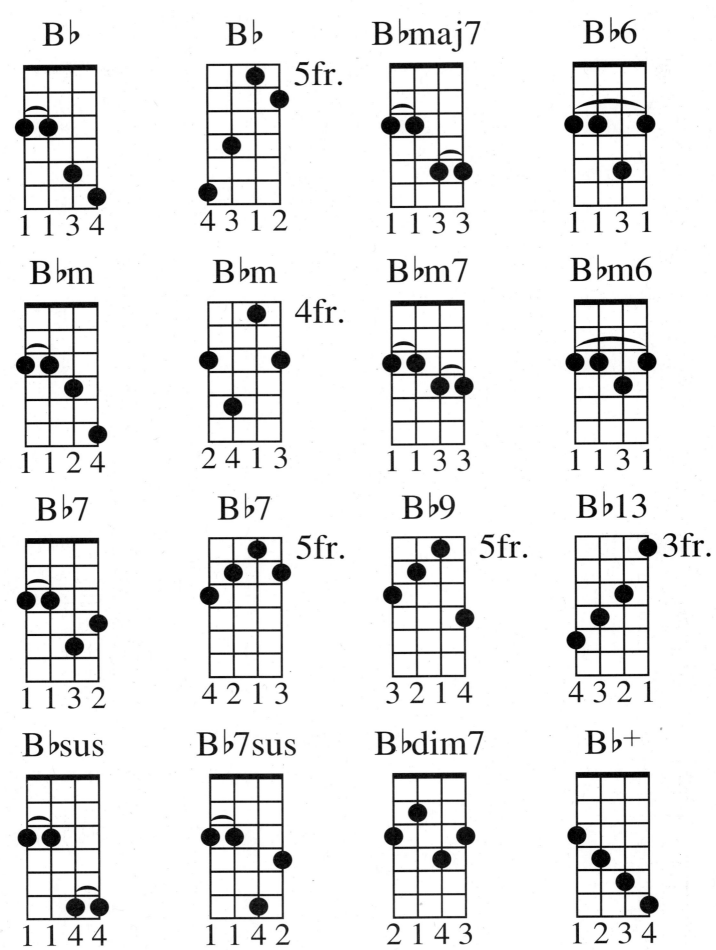

B CHORDS

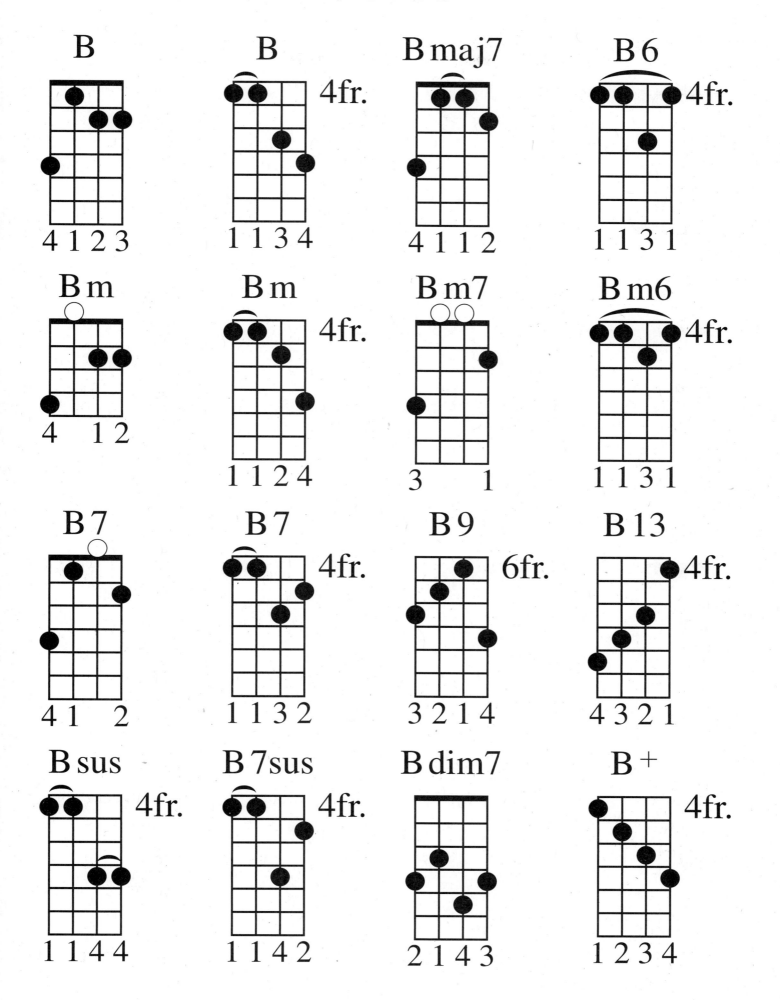

C CHORDS

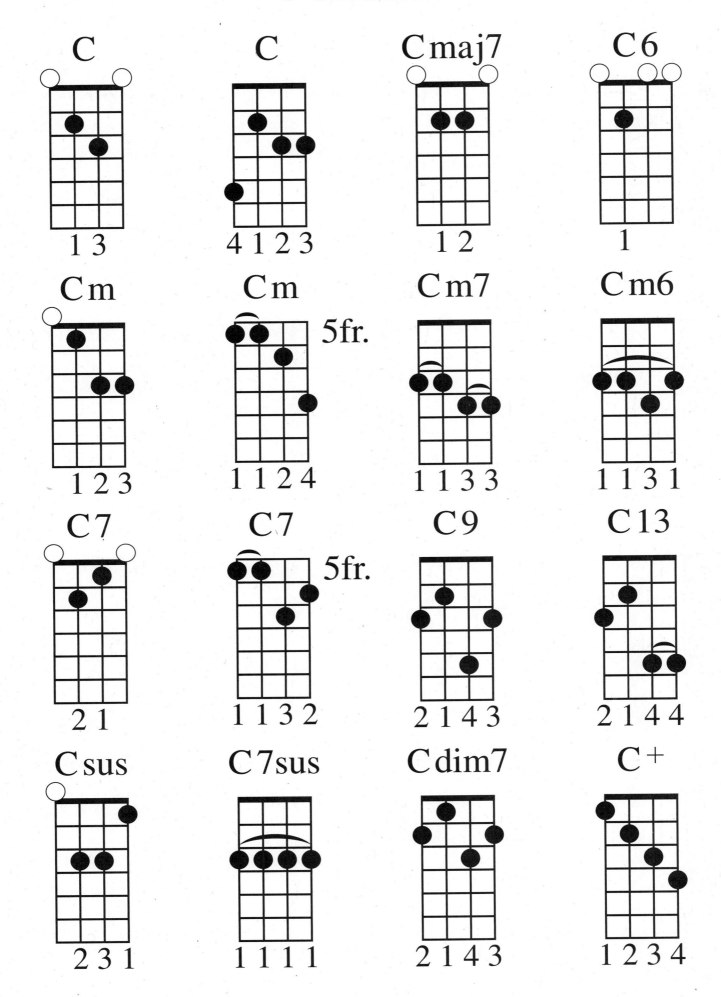

C♯ (D♭) CHORDS*

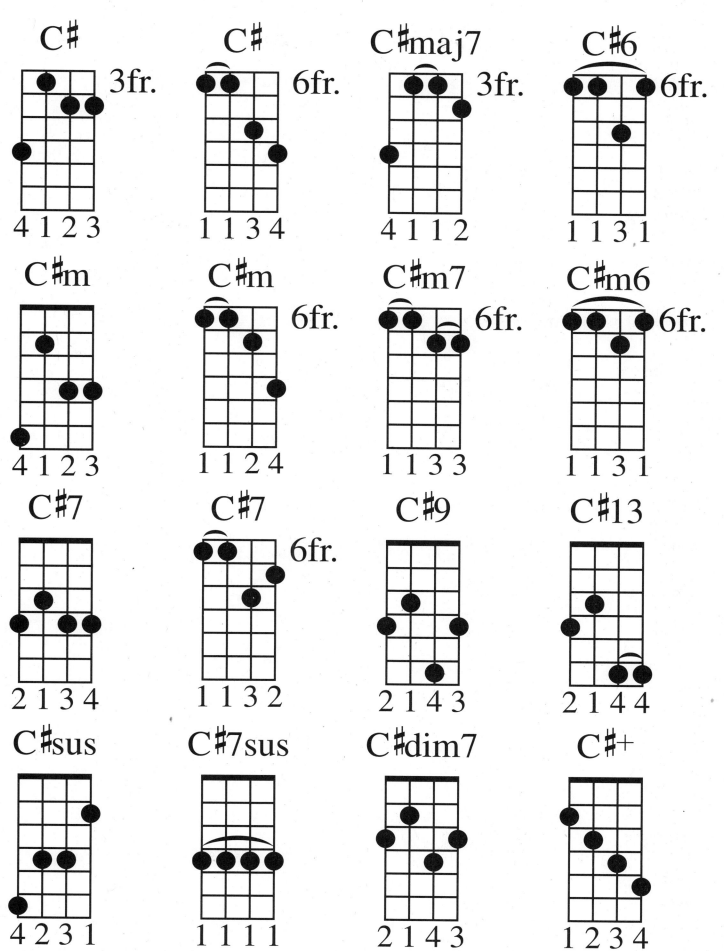

*C♯ and D♭ are two names for the same note.

D CHORDS

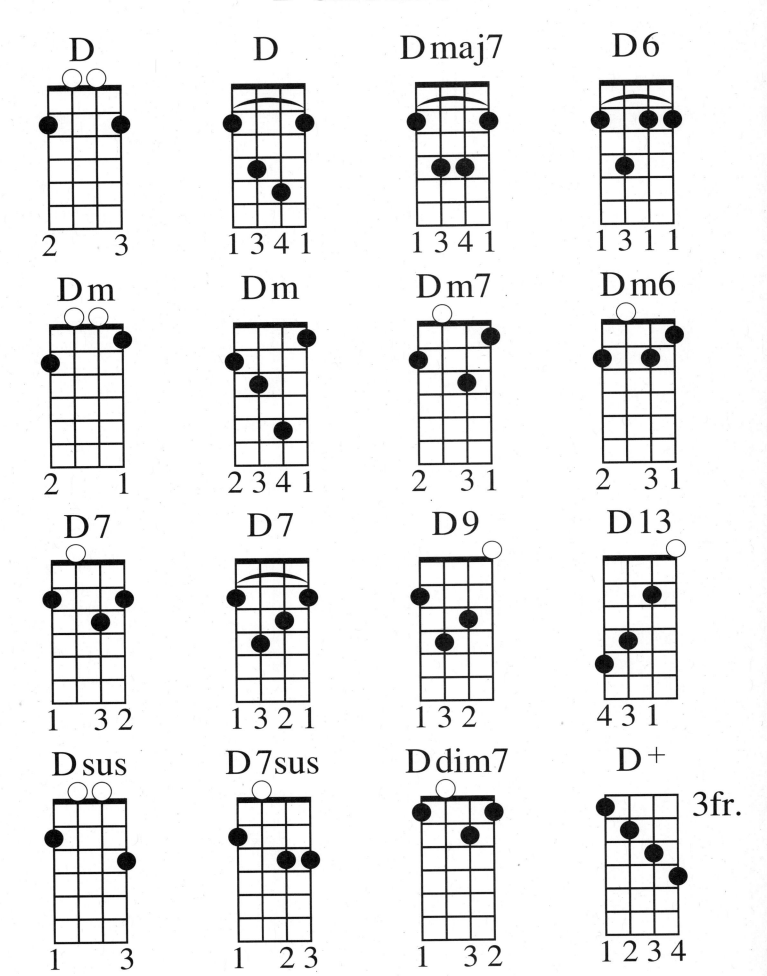

E♭ (D♯) CHORDS*

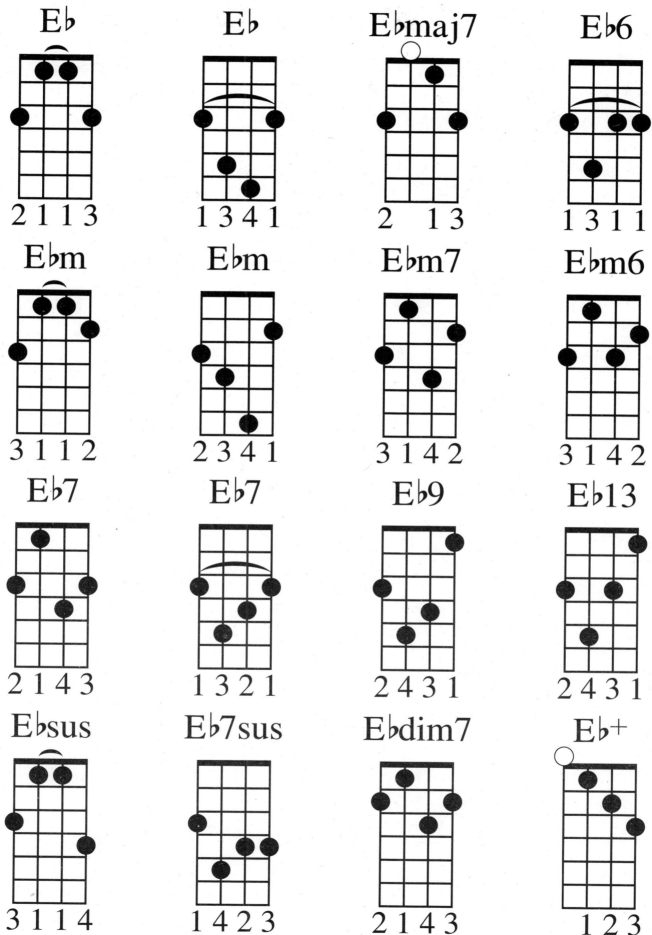

E♭   E♭   E♭maj7   E♭6

2 1 1 3   1 3 4 1   2 1 3   1 3 1 1

E♭m   E♭m   E♭m7   E♭m6

3 1 1 2   2 3 4 1   3 1 4 2   3 1 4 2

E♭7   E♭7   E♭9   E♭13

2 1 4 3   1 3 2 1   2 4 3 1   2 4 3 1

E♭sus   E♭7sus   E♭dim7   E♭+

3 1 1 4   1 4 2 3   2 1 4 3   1 2 3

*E♭ and D♯ are two names for the same note.

E CHORDS

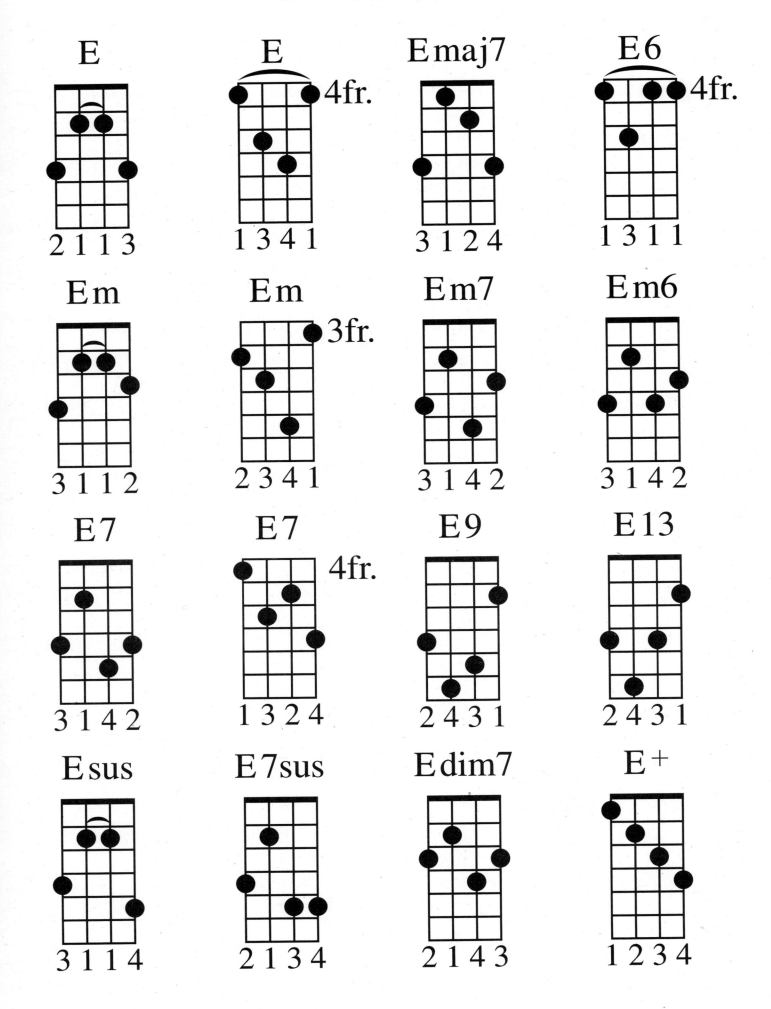

F CHORDS

57

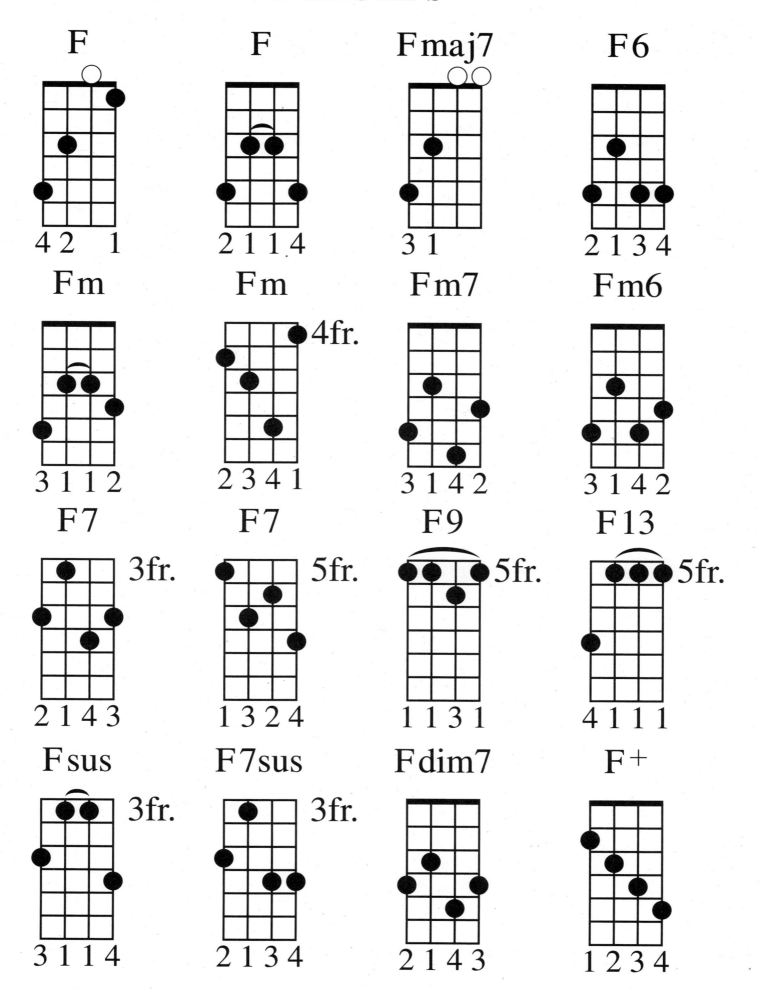

F# (G♭) CHORDS*

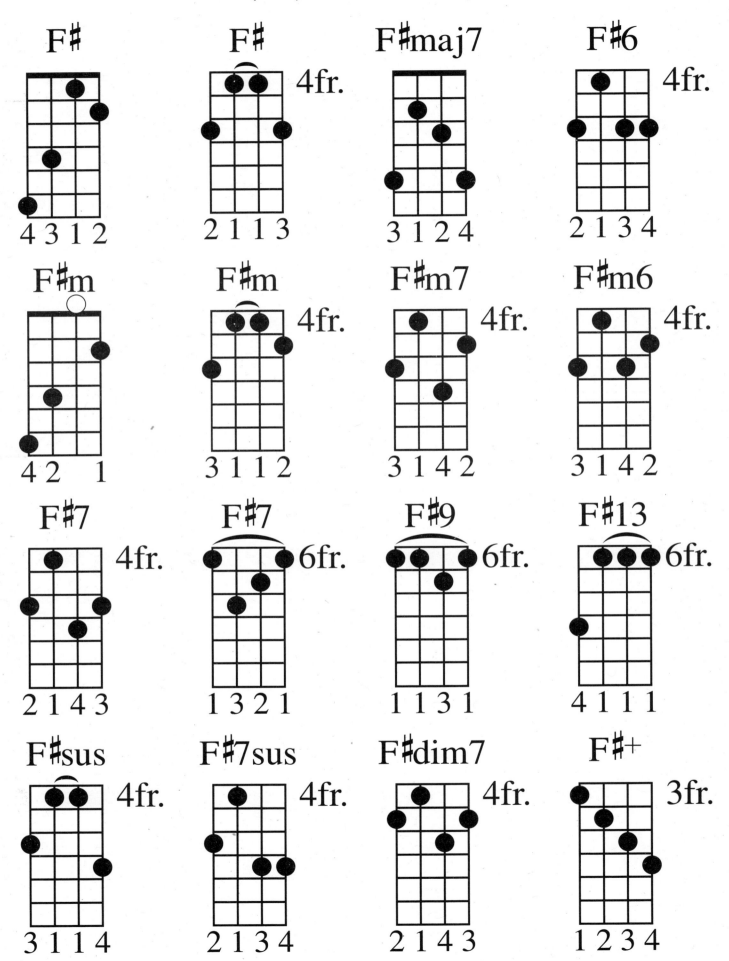

*F# and G♭ are two names for the same note.

G CHORDS

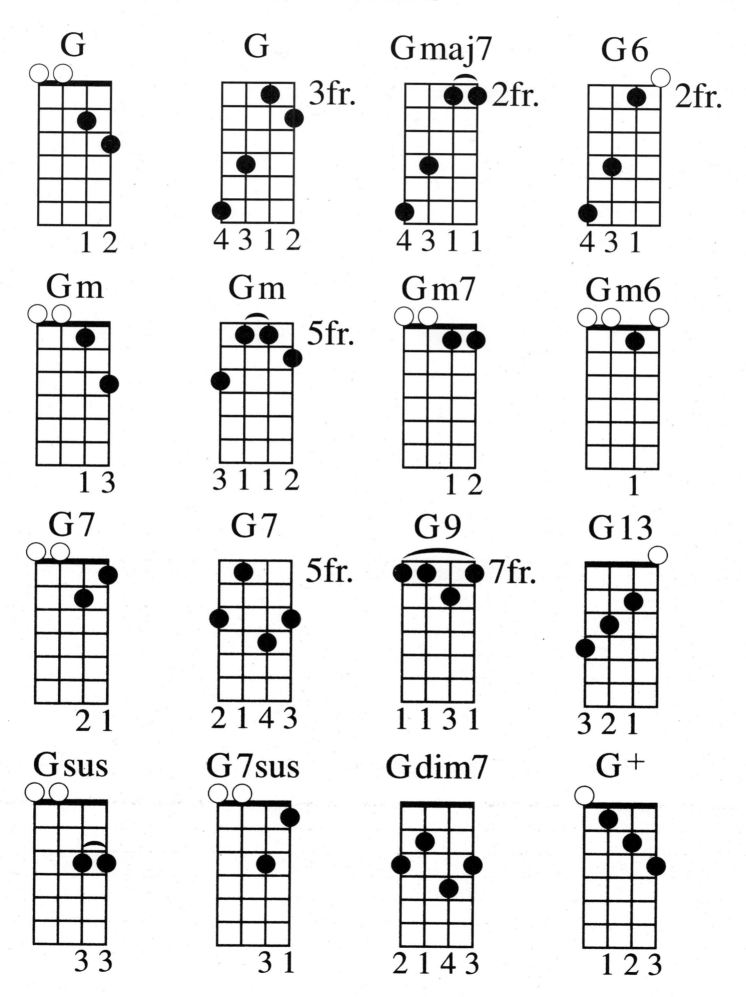

60

A♭ (G♯) CHORDS

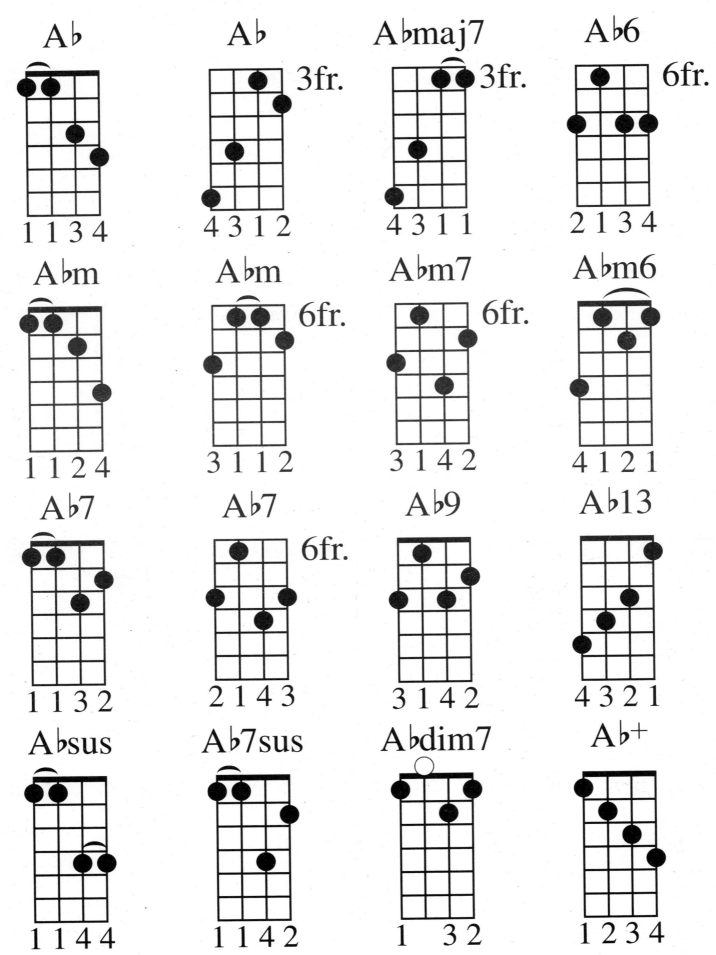

*A♭ and G♯ are two names for the same note.